MW01259457

2021

THROUGH MY MOTHER'S EYES

Melba T. Binion Sanders Johnson

KP PUBLISHING

Los Angeles

Copyright 2020 by Melba B. Johnson

All rights reserved. In accordance with the U.S. Copyright Act of 1976, the scanning, uploading, and electronic sharing of any part of this book without the permission of the publisher is unlawful piracy and theft of the author's intellectual property. If you would like to use material from this book (other than for review purposes), prior written permission must be obtained by contacting the publisher at info@knowledgepowerinc.com

Thank you for your support of the author's rights.

ISBN: 978-1-950936-55-7   (Hardcover)
ISBN: 978-1-950936-44-1   (Paperback)
ISBN: 978-1-950936-45-8   (Ebook)
Library of Congress Control Number: 2020917751

Editor:	Laurel J. Davis
Creator/Visionary:	Melba B. Johnson
Production Designer:	Chad Williams
Co-Producer:	Eloise Laws-Ivie
Photographer:	Moses Mitchell
Cover & Interior Designer:	Juan Roberts / Creative Lunacy
Literary Director:	Sandra L. Slayton

Published by

KP PUBLISHING

Publisher of Fiction, Nonfiction & Children's Books
Valencia, CA 91355
www.kp-pub.com

Printed in the United States of America

PROLOGUE

Open your eyes, look within.
Are you satisfied with the life you're living?
                                    —BOB MARLEY

C O N T

E   N   T   S

CONTENT NOTE:
The M-O-T-H-E-R Bridges
are quotes from talent in the docu-series
"Through My Mother's Eyes."

FROM THE
VISIONARY

MELBA T. BINION-SANDERS-JOHNSON

"One day, you'll be able to see through grandma's eyes."

These are the words my mother always spoke to my sibling and me when it came time to remind us to straighten up and fly right. They usually followed when there were frustrations on both sides, typical of parents and children trying to figure out life's issues. Sometimes with success, other times while waiting until I was truly able to look through my grandma's eyes.

How far you go in life depends on your being tender with the young, compassionate with the aged, sympathetic with the striving, and tolerant of the weak and strong. Because someday in your life, you will have been all of these. - George Washington Carver

When a woman is talking to you, listen to what she says with her EYES. - Victor Hugo

What did Victor Hugo indeed mean by this?

As young children, we depend on our moms for literally everything. Then, as teenagers, we want to do almost everything without them. And finally, as we become adults and parents ourselves and continue to get older, we realize the significance every mother always has. The multifaceted life of motherhood sometimes goes beyond the surface of what society can see. Oftentimes, it lies within the eyes of a mother.

Through My Mother's Eyes explores all the possibilities, the thoughts, and the ideas of how we view these special women in our everyday lives, pondering motherhood through their unique lens.

With simple expressions and beautifully captured photographic images, *Through My Mother's Eyes* focuses simply on the eyes and the stories and messages that emanate from within them. Based on the familiar adage, "The eyes are the key to the soul," this wonderful collection of images and quotes takes you on the pure journey of how the eyes speak everyone's truth—if we just look.

The individuals featured in these pages share what they see in the eyes of their mothers, or what their mothers would see in their own eyes, whether or not the relationship is biological. The photographs are captivating, drawing you in with their subtle intensity. They show how the eyes are indeed the gateway to the untold stories hinted at through the individual portraits of the different people featured and their compelling statements about what they see.

Through My Mother's Eyes gives people a platform to talk about who they are . . . and whose they are. The people we listen to and value in our lives make us who we are.

THE
JOURNEY

The journey of *Through My Mother's Eyes* manifested out of, first, a pure desire and, second, the actualization of that desire to recognize that I, at the beautiful age of 60, could finally see through my own mother's eyes. As a child, when I was faced with challenging situations or revelation of experiences, my mother would always say to me, "One day, you will be able to see through grandma's eyes." I didn't understand why she said that or what it truly meant.

As I grew, matured, married, and raised my own children and grandchildren, one day it hit me: Just live long enough and you will come to understand motherhood on your terms and feel the same pains and joys of life just like all the mothers before you. In other words, I would one day see life through their eyes.

That's why *Through My Mother's Eyes* matters so much to me. I am honoring those I have tried to emulate. I thought motherhood and even grand motherhood was something new that I had designed when I had children and then they had children. But I eventually came to realize that my actions, attitudes, and growing pains were nothing new in the world. When I stopped looking just within myself and my own experiences and perspectives on what it means to be a mother, when I finally really stepped outside of myself and looked into my mother's eyes, guess what? I saw me!

And it changed my world. From then on, I saw possibilities where I once saw fears, now no longer needing permission. Looking through my mother's eyes opened my own eyes, and I knew from that moment on that my daughters needed to know my truths and to know that it's always okay to try again. I wanted my children to always know that if at my age I can still change my world, then so can they. *Through My Mother's Eyes* is one way to impart that wisdom to them.

The selected individuals featured in this book show you just through their respective eyes what drives them to be who they are and where they are in life as opposed to just some happenstance being at the right place at the right time. In these photographs, I want you to connect with what you see in the eyes. Through the eyes, you see history, untold stories, and everyone in that person's life who wants to be seen.

And whether it's one person's eyes you connect with or everyone's, you will discover that we are all the same no matter how much any of us has or doesn't have. We are all the children of our mothers.

Unbeknownst to me, the journey of creating *Through My Mother's Eyes* was happening while I was on a completely different path to find words of wisdom and encouragement for one of my yoga students. Shalu, a beautiful lady, directed me to a book titled, The Artist Way (which I highly recommend). She said it helped her find her way back to a creative sense of self as well as with working out all the everyday madness that we as individuals encounter.

At the beginning of each year, I embark on a spiritual, empowering journey, check myself, and get my s--t together. The start of 2018 was as good a time as any to read this new book. I decided to take up the cause and join Shalu on a 12-week assignment to get to the other side of what I call my shift in life. As a yoga instructor, I describe the shifting process as, "Sometimes the teacher may become the student." Or, as my husband tells me, "Keep an open mind, you might learn something." Even more to the point is my favorite quote from my father, Tarlton Binion: "Just when you thought you knew it all, there is something else to learn." Thank you for that one, Dad. It has come in handy.

Within the first two weeks of my reading *The Artist Way*, things started to happen. Not only was I more alert, I began to notice things I never had before. I didn't recognize me. I have always felt I had a purpose, and I have always said to myself there is something I'm supposed to do in my life and when it shows up, I'll know. Well, Hello! For those 12 weeks, I would get up early every morning to do my assignments, enjoying the transformation I knew was always in me waiting to come out. I just needed a swift kick.

THAT SWIFT KICK SOON CAME.

My amazing mother and namesake, Melba Binion, raised seven children. She is 86 years old and still her memory never fails her. She can still remember and recite poems from her elementary school years in Birmingham, Alabama. Unfortunately, her health has not been kind to her, as she has diabetes. One particular afternoon Mother had a fall and went to the hospital, but thank goodness, she was able to go home the next day. I brought her lunch from one of her favorite fish markets and we started having our usual conversation about the grandkids and catching up on their activities. About nine minutes into our chat, while Mother was talking, her lips were still moving but no words were coming out. I immediately thought, Oh no! She's had a stroke! I calmed myself so as not to frighten her, and I just sat still.

Sitting there with her, I began to focus on Mother's eyes. Suddenly, out of nowhere, those eyes spoke to me! There was this personal dialogue her eyes were having with me, filled with warmth and passion and stories and concerns, but it was the most intimate non-audible conversation in my life with her. They were saying, "I pray your life is full. I want you to be happy. There are no rule books on how to be a good mother. I wish I could run and jump and do the things that the number 86 does not allow. How do I tell you all the things that my lips have held back?" And so on.

I sat there in awe. At that very moment, the statement my mother used to always say to me suddenly registered within me: "One day, you will be able to see through grandma's eyes." However, after a few moments I just stood up and shook it off. I wasn't sure if she had a stroke, or if I had hallucinated. I also wasn't sure if I needed to mention it to my siblings or my husband. I held onto it and let it mull around and simmer within my soul first, primarily because I didn't know what to do with it.

THEN IT HAPPENED AGAIN.

Not with my mother this time but with a long-time associate and friend. In fact, all of the circumstances were completely different from those of my experience with my mother. But I vividly recall what happened. I was attending a commercial casting call and was sitting waiting for my turn to audition. I had just come off of an intense workshop the prior week on "How to Book the Job." So, I was pumped, focused, and even had a bank deposit slip in my back pocket ready to book the job. I also had my agent on speed dial, just knowing I would later call and say, "Let me know when the call-back is." When I was told I was next, I was instructed to go down the hall where my audition would be after the woman on deck.

FROM THE VISIONARY
MELBA T. BINION-SANDERS-JOHNSON Cont

When that woman auditioning before me turned around, I recognized her immediately. It was Freda Payne, singer, songstress, and yogi like me. We practiced together for more than 30 years, but I had not seen her at an audition in years. Freda recognized me as well, and we exchanged greetings. Our conversation had only briefly begun when suddenly, while she was speaking to me, her lips were moving, but no words were coming out.

"Oh my goodness! It's me!" I thought to myself. I immediately settled into Freda's eyes and knew there was a message. Sure enough, her eyes began to speak of her career and where she is today. Now, I am not sure to this day if those non-verbal "talks" were my self-imposed thoughts or what. But it was enough to recognize something was going on here and I had to pay attention. Within minutes, Freda's eyes had expressed so much to me that I was blown away, and then within seconds, her audible voice returned with, "Good luck on your casting."

I was mystified. In fact, immediately afterwards, I couldn't focus on my dialogue for the audition, and when I did, I couldn't remember my lines. So much for booking the job and the deposit slip in my back pocket. Now, how ironic that, when I started this *Through My Mother's Eyes* book project, all I seemed to see on television was the commercial I barely auditioned for, over and over again. Maybe I went to the audition, not to "book the job," but to be in sync with what I was really supposed to be doing.

That night, I dreamt of my mother. So begins my journey of looking through the eyes, and so begins the journey of this book, *Through My Mother's Eyes*. You will see people you know, people you don't know, and people you need to know. Welcome!

×

PURPOSE
AND
NEED

Everyone faces crises in life where they will need adequate advice and inspiration. These pivotal times are part of our individual growth. ***Through My Mother's Eyes*** serves as a reminder for people to maintain their faith in their own journeys, and that purpose comes from learning. Surprisingly and in touching ways, written in a conversational style that evokes solid storytelling, ***Through My Mother's Eyes*** is both a celebration of individuality and a tribute to the common spirit of all mothers.

Through My Mother's Eyes

THE COLLECTION

"REMEMBER WHO YOU ARE, AND WHOSE YOU ARE."

—Melba Fitzpatrick Binion

"WHEN I LOOK INTO MY MOTHER'S EYES,

I
SEE
ME."

—Melba T. Binion-Sanders-Johnson

"When I look into my mother's eyes, I'd tell her, don't worry about what other people think."

—Alexandria Sanders-Yates

"I SEE MY MOTHER AS A SALVE ... A BALM.

I SEE
THAT PLACE
IN THE WORLD
FOR HER.
SHE IS
SOMEONE WHO
HEALS OTHERS
AND IS
COMPASSIONATE
BUT NEEDS
HEALING HERSELF
AS WELL."

—Chelsea W. Sanders

Through My Mother's Eyes

"BE KIND AND BRAVE."

—Kelsey Yates

"To be educated, have a good life."

—*Skyler Yates*

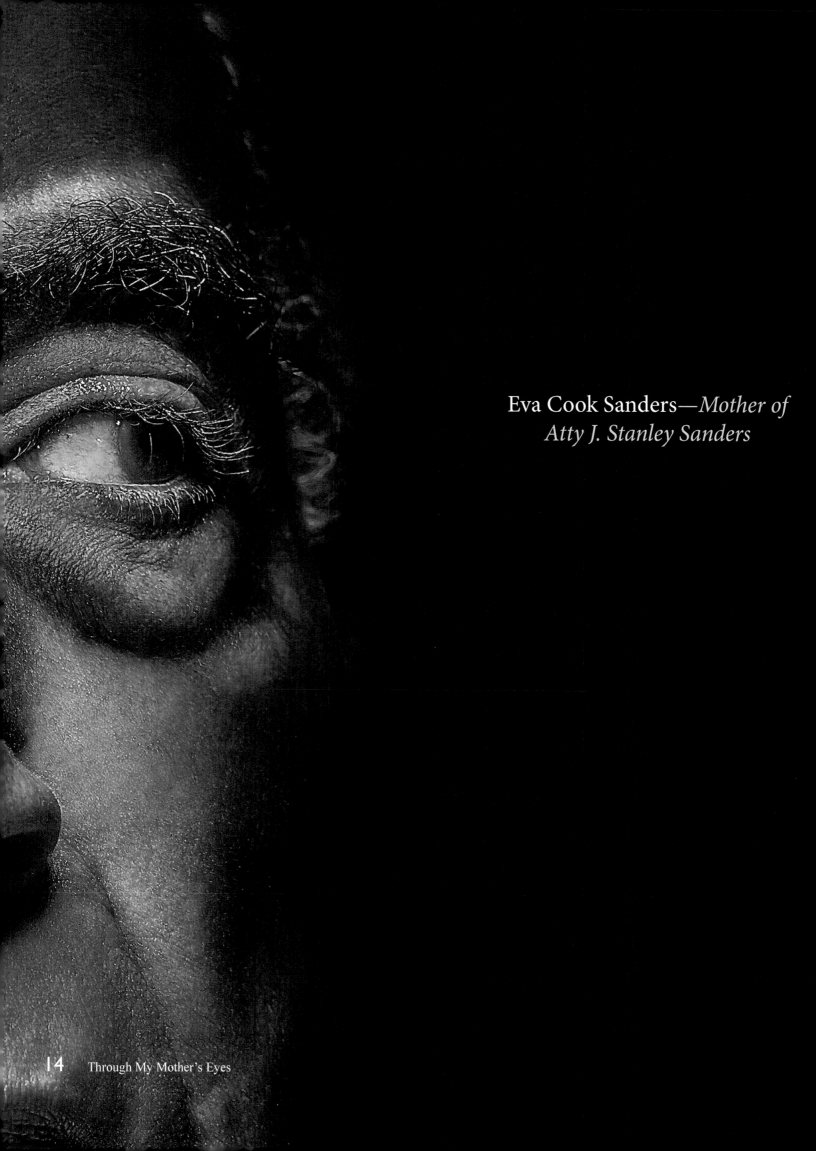

Eva Cook Sanders—*Mother of*
Atty J. Stanley Sanders

"She would say, 'Well done and thank you for understanding the importance of the legacy you were born to build on and to continue.'"

—*Attorney J. Stanley Sanders*

"IF SHE
WAS
LOOKING
INTO
MY
EYES,

SHE WOULD SEE
THAT **HER SON**
HAS MORE OF HER
QUALITIES
THAN SHE WOULD THINK,
LOVING
MY WIFE
THE WAY
I SAW MY DAD
LOVED HER."

—*Bernard William Kinsey*

"I don't remember my Mother's Eyes, she died when I was two. But I remember MY FATHER'S MOTHER'S EYES, who raised me. Those mother's eyes were STRONG, yet GENTLE. They SHOWED STRENGTH even though she did not talk a lot.

I SAW
THIS
IN
HER
EYES."

—Shirley Kinsey

"WHEN I
LOOK INTO
MY MOTHER'S EYES,
I SEE LOVE,
CONCERN AND
DEVOTION.
SHE MADE SURE
THE FAMILY
STAYED TOGETHER
AND WAS
THE STAPLE."

—*Michael F. Johnson*

Cloteal Elizabeth Johnson,
—*Mother of Michael F. Johnson*

"I TRIED TO BE THE PERSON THAT I **TRULY** AM, BUT ALSO THE PERSON THAT **MY MOTHER AND FATHER** WANTED ME TO BE."

—*Diane Watson,*
Retired Congresswoman

"SHE WAS SHY AND INSECURE BUT BLOSSOMED INTO A POWERHOUSE, AN A-TYPE PERSONALITY AND BECAME A PRISON WARDEN. 'SHE WAS SOMETHING ELSE,' JERRY BROWN ONCE SAID OF HER."

—Senator Holly Mitchell

"LOOKING THROUGH MY MOTHER'S EYES, I SEE BEAUTY, WISDOM, AND LIGHT."

—Lita Gaithers Owens

Through My Mother's Eyes

"LOOKING THROUGH MY MOTHER'S EYES, I SEE LOVE OF GOD AND FAMILY."

—Dorothy Gaithers

"My Mother has an IMPACT on how I walk and relate to people. She knew how to get inside my head without saying anything.

—Pamela Warner

"I KNOW YOU SHOULD DEFINITELY BE PROUD OF ME, AND YOU, MOTHER, SHOULD BE EXTREMELY PROUD OF YOURSELF. ... IT IS BECAUSE OF YOU."

—Malcolm Jamal Warner

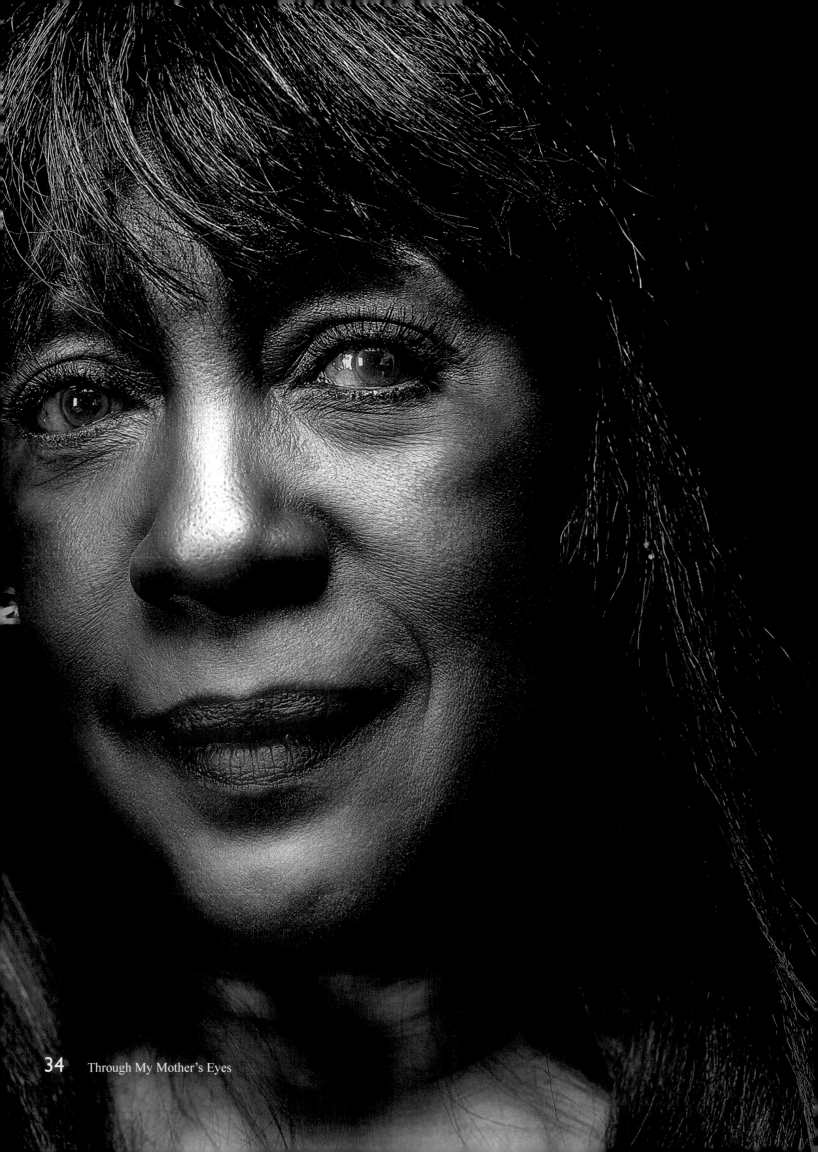

Through My Mother's Eyes

"Looking into my Mother's Eyes, I would see she was VERY, VERY PROUD of ME as her daughter. I could SEE HAPPINESS."

—*Mary Wilson*

"LOOKING INTO MY MOTHER'S EYES, SHE WOULD ALWAYS SAY: 'ALWAYS MAINTAIN CONTACT WITH YOUR SISTER, BECAUSE SHE LOVES YOU.'"

—*Freda Payne*

Through My Mother's Eyes

"I THINK
MY MOM WOULD SAY,
'YOU GO GIRL,
YOU DID IT,
YOU DIDN'T LET
ANYONE STOP YOU!'
COLOR COATED
CASTING
WAS HER TERM.
MY MOM WOULD
NOT LET THAT
LIMIT US."

—*Judy Pace*

"My Mother would always say: 'Nobody else is better than you.'

For me, 'If a man does not seek humility, HUMILITY WILL SEEK THE MAN.'"

—*Bill Duke*

Through My Mother's Eyes

"If I were looking into my Mother's eyes right now, I would see **Wisdom, Compassion, Smarts, Kindness** and **Caring.** That's where I learned to care about others from my Mother and how I learned to **pay things forward.**"

—*Beverly Todd*

"MY MOM WAS SHORT FIESTY, MAYBE 5 FEET. MY MOTHER WAS A BANNING ROOSTER, SHE MIGHT HAVE BEEN SMALL, BUT SHE WAS BIG, SHE DIDN'T BACK DOWN OFF OF NOBODY. SHE WAS STERN.

SHE LOOKED AT ME IN MY EYES IN DIFFERENT STAGES. WHEN I WAS YOUNG, IT WOULD BE JUST GET A GOOD JOB. LATER ON WHEN I GOT OLDER, GET A JOB AND GET MARRIED. THEN WHEN I BECAME AN ACTOR, SHE LOOKED AT ME IN FEAR. SHE DIDN'T WANT ANYONE TO MAKE ME LESS THAN WHO I WAS.

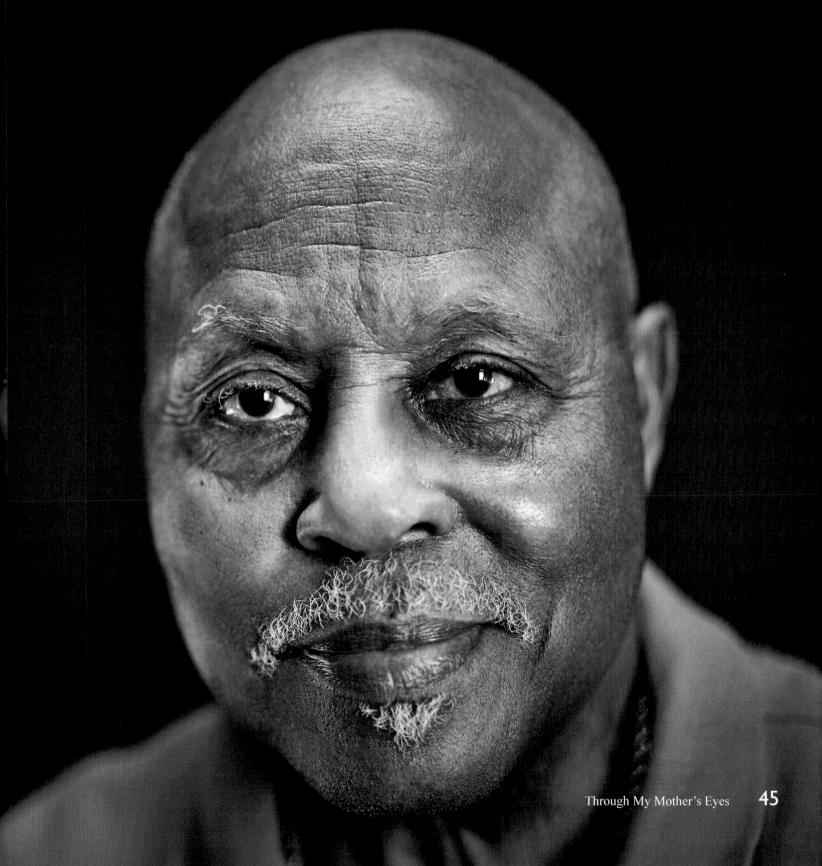

LAST TIME SHE LOOKED AT ME WITH AWE. . . THAT I HAD MADE IT."

—Roger E. Mosley

"My Mother was a Giver, a Nurturer and didn't expect anything in return."

—*Dr. Gail Jackson*

"My life parallels with my mother's, the way **SHE DEALT** with **PEOPLE** and **TALKED** to **THEM**. She was a loving, sharing and caring person when it came to people."

—*Dr. Keith Richardson*

"HER EYES
WERE **ALLURING,**
WHOLESOME
AND SHOWED
A LOVING
SOUL.
WHEN I WOULD
GO ASTRAY,
SHE WOULD
REEL ME IN."

—Kathleen Bradley

"I WOULD CALL HER **MEAN MILLY**, BECAUSE SHE WAS TOUGH. MY MOTHER DID NOT TELL ME OFTEN THAT SHE LOVED ME, BUT SHE DIDN'T HAVE TO, I KNEW IT."

—*Iris Gordy*

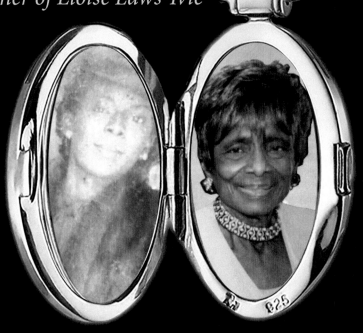

Miola Laws
- *Mother of Eloise Laws-Ivie*

"MOM, YOU HAVE BEEN MY MOTIVATION AND INSPIRATION. YOU HAVE BEEN THERE WITH ME WHEN I WAS AT MY LOWEST AND THERE WHEN I WAS RIDING HIGH. YOU ALWAYS HAD ANSWERS WHEN I NEEDED ONE. AS A MOM YOU DON'T JUST GET THE EASY STUFF BUT, YOU GET IT ALL. THANK YOU."

—*Eloise Laws-Ivie*

"My Mother would always speak words that I needed to hear to build up my spirit. Hoping that I would achieve just a portion of what she thought I could do."

—*Attorney Rickey Ivie*

"MY MOTHER
HAS SUCH A WAY
OF LOVING.
WHEN
I SEE MY DAUGHTER,
I SEE SUCH
AMBITION TO
HER FAMILY
AND A
VERY STRONG
WOMAN
IN MY BABY GIRL."

—*Glodean White*

"IN
MY MOTHER'S EYES
SHE WAS
VERY SUPPORTIVE
OF HER CHILDREN.
I LEARNED
TO BE THE
STRONG PERSON
I AM TODAY,
HOW TO RECEIVE LOVE
AND GET IT,
BECAUSE OF HER
AND THE WAY
SHE TAUGHT ME."

—Shaherah White

"My Mother didn't raise me. When I looked into her eyes, I saw a sad person. She was fearful. But when we did finally get together she said, 'About time you got home, boy, Welcome home.'"

—Roland Bynum

Through My Mother's Eyes

"HER EYES SPOKE STRENGTH AND COMPASSION. IF IT HADN'T BEEN FOR **ESTHER BYRD,** I DON'T KNOW WHERE I WOULD BE. SHE LEFT A **LEGACY OF LOVE."**

—*Petri H. Byrd*

"I WOULD
HAVE TO TELL HER
HOW MUCH
I LOVED HER
AND HOW
BEAUTIFUL
AND STRONG
SHE WAS
TO RAISE SIX CHILDREN.
BUT I WOULD
ALSO REMEMBER WHEN
SHE CALLED ME PATRICIA,
I KNEW I WAS IN TROUBLE,
THAT'S WHY I LOVE
TO BE CALLED BONNIE."

—*Bonnie Pointer*

Through My Mother's Eyes

"I WAS SHAPED AND MOLDED BY BOTH MY PARENTS, EDUCATOR AND FARMER. WE WERE PRIVILEGED, GROWING UP IN THE SOUTH OF SEGREGATION, BUT WE STILL HAD THE OPPORTUNITY TO LEARN DUE TO MY MOTHER AND FATHER, THINGS SUCH AS, BASIC FUNDAMENTALS OF LIFE, AND HOW TO ACHIEVE, AND EXCEL. IT WAS THEN UP TO US TO MAKE IT WORK FOR US."

—*Peggy Williams*

"She is a combination of people. My mother, my best friend, my number one advisor. The one who raised me. She is the person when you are on the top of the mountain you want to call. She is the one who, when you are in the gutter, she's the one you want to call. She's the one."

—Bill Johnson

"She is an INSPIRATION to her sons. She taught us a lot of things she learned on a farm that *her father owned*—109 acres. We had chores that molded us. She was an inspiration to our friends and a LOT of others' lives."

—*Marcus Williams*

Through My Mother's Eyes

"**I** WILL HAVE ALREADY
TOLD HER
ALL SHE NEEDS TO KNOW
AND **MOST**
IMPORTANTLY,
THAT
I LOVE HER."

—*Lydia Cincore Templeton*

"My
Mother
would
always say,
Pretty is
as pretty
does,
and
Pretty is
from
inside
out."
—Dr. Pamela Wiley

"She would tell me, 'You are gonna be **ALRIGHT**,' and I would tell her now, Mom, I have done **JUST FINE.**"

—*Silvia Drew Ivie*

"There is
not a day that goes by
that I do not think of my
Mother. I see her in
EVERY BLESSING
that GOD HAS MANIFESTED
in my life."

—*Tina Treadwell*

"THERE ARE
TWO PAIRS OF EYES.
FIRST, MY BIOLOGICAL MOTHER'S
EYES, THE ONES THAT DID NOT
RAISE ME BUT
WHICH HELD A LOT OF
PAIN, SORROW AND A LOT
OF REGRETS.
THEN THERE ARE
MY ADOPTED MOTHER'S
EYES, THAT SHOWED
ME JOY, AMBITION AND
CREATIVITY.
THESE ARE FILLED WITH THE
LOVE OF GOD.
THE COMBINATION OF THE
TWO, I GOT WHAT I NEEDED
FROM BOTH."

—Gloria Lockhart

Through My Mother's E

"I REALIZED THROUGH MY JOURNEY THAT MY MOTHER WAS MY FIRST EDUCATOR."

—Ron Brown

"LOOKING INTO MY MOTHER'S EYES I WOULD IMMEDIATELY CHANGE PREPARED TO PREPARING TO CALL ME, 'BABY BOY.' I SAW PAIN AND VIOLENCE IN HER EYES, WHICH WERE ALWAYS AT ODDS.'"

—Tony King

"If I were looking into my Mother's Eyes, I would see the message of, Every Tragedy is a Triumph. My Mother built me to be an artist and my mom left me this gift."

—Skyler Grey

Kristin High
—Mother of Skyler Grey

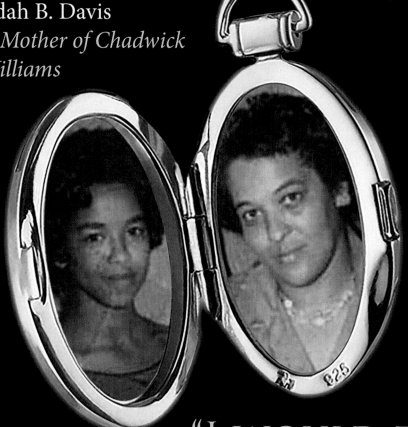

Adah B. Davis
—*Mother of Chadwick Williams*

Zerline Williams
—*Grandmother of Chadwick Williams*

"I WOULD TELL
MY MOM,
I CAN'T WAIT
TO GET TO HEAVEN,
BECAUSE I HAVE
SO MANY
QUESTIONS
FOR YOU."

—*Chadwick L. Williams*

Through My Mother's Eyes

"IF I WERE EVER TO
SLIP AWAY,
I WAS TO GO TO BE
WITH MY FAMILY;
WHICH DID NOT
REGISTER
WHEN WE WERE YOUNG,
BUT AS
WE
GREW
OLDER,
WE
UNDERSTOOD."

—*Rev. Cecil Murray*

Through My Mother's Eyes

"THAT LADY WAS A CHARACTER. I LOOKED IN THE MIRROR AFTER SHE PASSED AWAY AND I REALIZED, 'DAMN I LOOK JUST LIKE HER.' SHE WAS 15 WHEN SHE HAD ME, AND MY MOTHER AND GRANDMOTHER RAISED ME. MY MOM WAS SOMEBODY BECAUSE OF HER VALUES."

—Clinton Jones

Through My Mother's Eyes

"'OPEN YOUR MOUTH, SING THAT SONG,' SHE WOULD TELL ME WHEN I WOULD SING AS A CHILD. SHE WAS MY FIRST VOCAL COACH. *LOVE'S IN NEED OF LOVE TODAY*, A STEVIE WONDER SONG, THAT WAS OUR SONG. MY MOTHER AND I. SHE WAS A STRONG LADY, EVEN THOUGH I WAS EXPOSED TO HER PAINS OF GROWING UP WITH HER FATHER, SHE WAS ALWAYS ON PURPOSE WITH ME.

THE LAST TIME I LOOKED INTO HER EYES, SHE WANTED ME TO KNOW THAT SHE WAS HAPPY WITH ME. I WOULD TELL HER, IF SHE WAS LOOKING INTO MY EYES, I AM FINE NOW. SHE ALLOWED ME TO FEEL ALL THE LOVE FROM WHEREVER SHE WAS AT WHEN SHE CAME TO VISIT. WHEN SHE DIED, SHE SAID TO ME, 'I GOT MY BABY BACK.'"

—*Steve Russell*

"My ride or die, my rib, my Mother is a spit fire, she is a DYNAMIC AND AMAZING WOMAN. She gave me my Strength, made me know early in life that my voice is powerful. When I look at her, I see a woman of strength but also a woman who made extreme sacrifices for her kids and family. Her blessing and gift have created WHO I AM TODAY."

—*Sharon Polk*

unapologetically

"My Mother would tell me, 'I couldn't have asked for a better son,' and The Lord Blesses you so much because you are so good to your Mother."

—Don B. Welch

Through My Mother's Eyes

"My Mom has always been JOYOUS, JUBLIANT, and always placed importance on enjoying life at any cost. Always a vast imagination, which is a great balance in the world. When it is not necessarily always bright but continues to be a beacon of JOY. She would see in my Eyes the appreciation of HER to freely express my ideas in whatever medium is fit for me."

—Brook D'Leau

"SHE WAS THE ONLY ONE TO CARRY ME WHEN I COULD NOT DO IT FOR MYSELF."

—*Kimberly Dotson*

"I SEE
IN MY
MOTHER'S EYES,
EMOTIONAL
CARING,
LOVE.
I SEE GENTLENESS
A LEGACY
OF FRUIT
OF A PEOPLE."

—*Robin Rochelle*

Through My Mother's Eyes

"My Mother was **VERY STRONG** but she was very happy and proud of us. **My daughter** is **VERY CARING** and **GENEROUS** and we can **ALWAYS DEPEND** on **HER** for friendship and love."

—*Joyce Matthews*

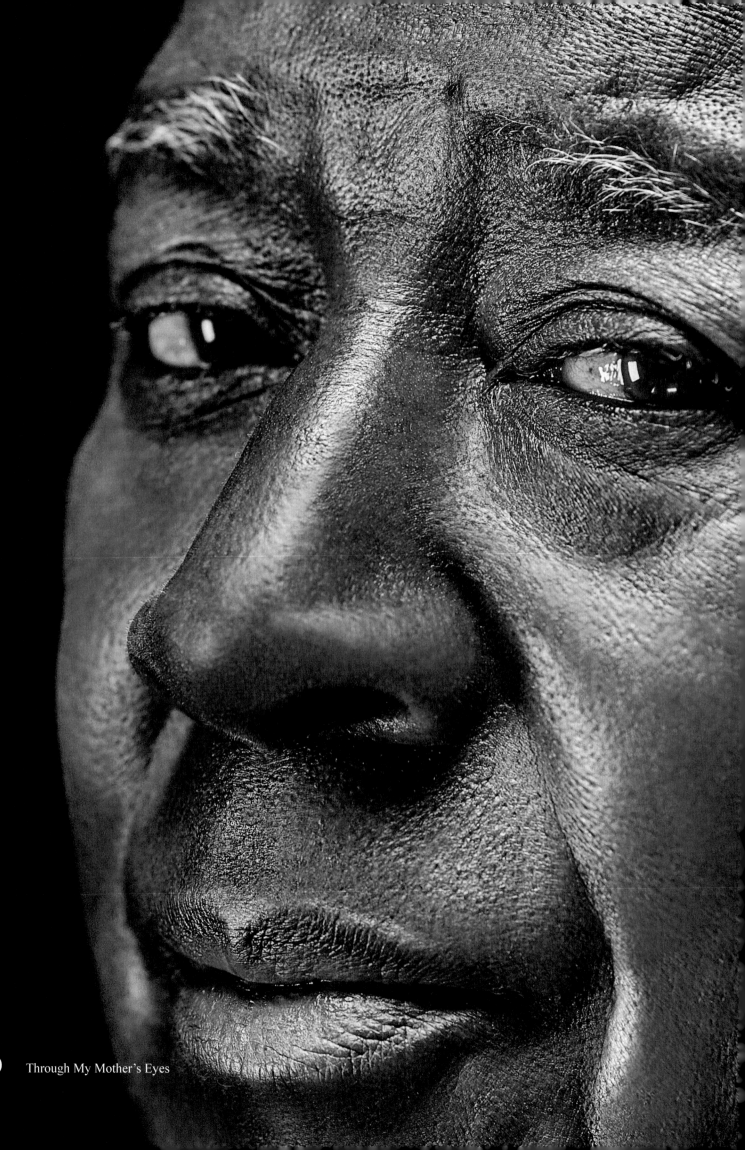

Through My Mother's Eyes

"LOOKING INTO MY MOTHER'S EYES I WOULD SEE

JOY.

I NEVER SAW MY MOTHER SAD OR UNHAPPY, **HER KIDS KEPT HER HAPPY.** IF SHE WERE LOOKING INTO MY EYES, SHE WOULD SEE HOW MUCH I CARED ABOUT HER AND

SHE WAS ALWAYS GOOD TO ME."

—*Jimmy Williams*

"IF I WERE TO
LOOK INTO
HER EYES,
I WOULD TELL HER
I AM LIVING
MY LIFE OUT
LOUD,
AUTHENTICALLY LIVING
MY BEST LIFE."

—*Gwendolyn Priestley*

"Two Moms raised me, the one with **Alzheimer** later on in life who was sad and mischievous.

Whereas the one I grew up with was JOYOUS, HAPPY and DELIGHTFUL.

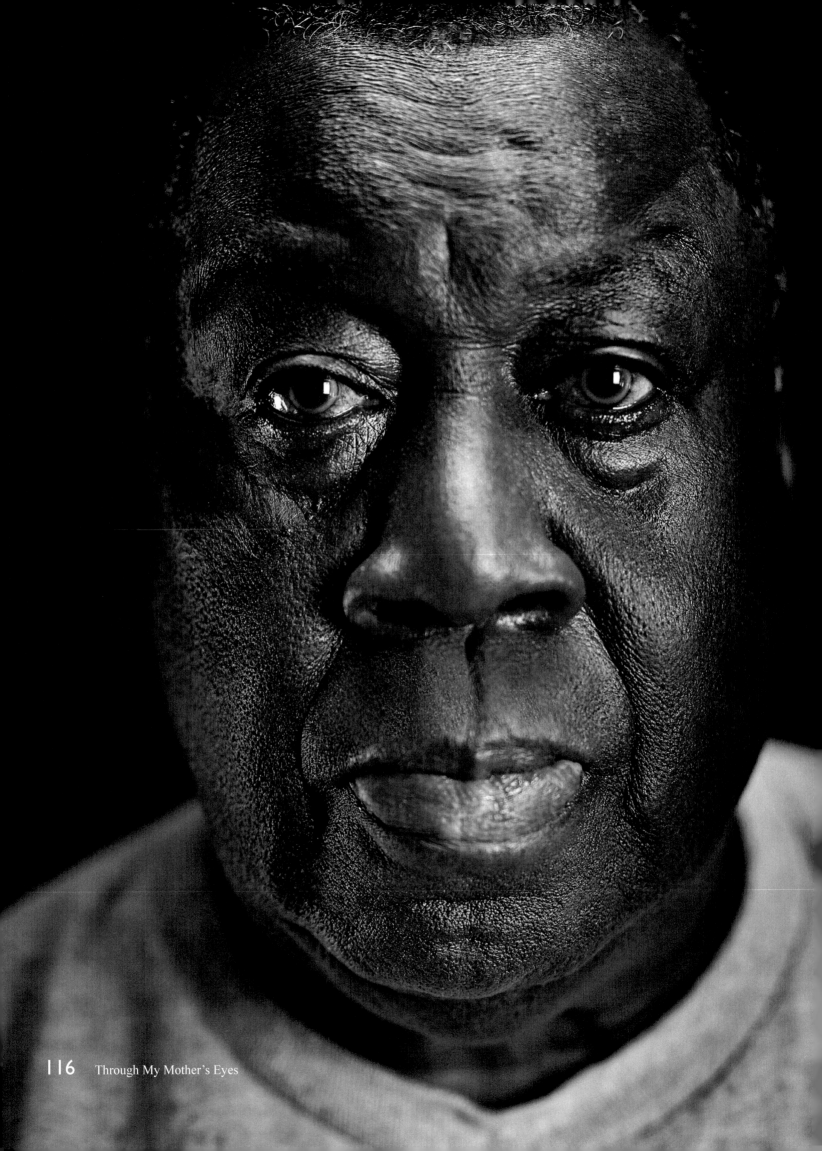

Through My Mother's Eyes

"She would say, 'Be Happy because there is someone out there worse off than you.' and 'Always wear clean underwear.' She would say 'boy, don't run from me, I'll kill you.' I was a bad boy."

—H.B. Barnum

Through My Mother's Eyes

"My Mother was My Number One Girl, she would always tell me, 'The world is yours, grab it by the tail and shake the mess out of it.'"

—*Councilman Herb Wesson*

"MY MOTHER WOULD SAY, 'IF YOU'VE GOT AN EDUCATION, YOU'VE GOT A CALLING CARD AND YOU GOT A GOOD START.'"

—*C.Z. Wilson*

Through My Mother's Eyes

"IN MY MOTHER'S EYES I SAW A VERY STRONG WOMAN, SHE DID IT ALL. SHE IS ALWAYS AS STRONG AS I KNEW HER TO BE.

HER EYES HAVE ALWAYS BEEN APPRECIATIVE. I TAKE CARE OF HER AND I CALL HER A KEPT WOMAN. SHE WOULD SAY, 'EVERYTHING HAS A PLACE AND IS IN ITS PLACE.'"

—*Vanessa Bell Calloway*

Through My Mother's Eyes

"THANK YOU FOR LIVING ON IN MY DAUGHTER, I GOT TO SEE YOU AGAIN. SHE LEFT ME IN GOOD HANDS."

—Zuri A. Murrell

"LOOKING INTO MY MOTHER'S EYES, SHE WOULD BE PROUD OF ME. MY LIFE HAS COME FULL CIRCLE. SHE WAS ONE OF THE SMARTEST PEOPLE I KNEW, INSISTED THAT WE HAD KNOWLEDGE AND DIDN'T EVEN GO TO COLLEGE HERSELF."

—Michael Colyar

Mama Jessie—*Mother of Adai Lamar*

"It's hard to see my mother as she has changed with memory loss. But the good thing is, I don't see the fear in her anymore. Because of what she saw when she was growing up, she has now forgotten and made peace with it..."

—*Adai Lamar*

"My Grandmother's and Mother's PRAYERS got me through life and a lot of challenges. **Her Happiest in my Eyes was her family.** I want her to see how I purposely implemented what she taught me. **Be mindful of how you care for yourself,** have pride and despite your circumstance, KEEP YOUR DREAMS GOING."

—*Cidney Allen Hollis*

"I MET MY
BIRTH MOTHER WHEN
I WAS 25. THE FIRST
THING I REALIZED WHEN
I SAW HER WAS THAT I
LOOK LIKE MY MOTHER.
WHEN I SAW HER, SHE
WAS LOOKING FOR
ABSOLUTION BUT
I DIDN'T HAVE IT.
I WAS RAISED BY
MY FATHER'S OTHER LADY, BUT
I AM GOOD, I COULDN'T BE
BETTER, ALL THE THINGS THAT
CAME MY WAY SHAPED ME.
I DON'T FEEL
BAD FOR ANY OF THE
TURBULENCE. IT MADE
ME A BETTER FATHER."

—*Jamie Benson*

"My Mother would say, reflecting back on her life, that she made mistakes." Her tears were of joy as she witnessed the fruits of her sacrafices and labor. "Your guidance and protection to us is priceless. Thanks Mom!"

—*Mary Louise King–Guinn*

Although I do not see,

"I SEE THROUGH MY MOTHER'S EYES."

—*Melba T. Binion-Sanders-Johnson*

THROUGH MY MOTHER'S EYES
ACKNOWLEDGMENTS

To my children, you keep me grounded and remind me of all of life's possibilities every single day. Your passion for life and your families reminds me of a job well done.

To my husband, Michael Ford Johnson, who would quietly encourage me and, when I wasn't around, would boast to the moon and back of my accomplishments. We all have our way of doing things, but I hear you loud and clear, and it happened because you let me be me.

This book would never have happened without my two partners. To Eloise Laws-Ivie, who saw my vision and believed in it as much as I did and said, "No matter what, we are going to make this happen." And to Chad Williams, who wore every possible hat necessary to make this project come to life, from filling in the gaps as photographer, videographer, artist, businessman—you name it, he did it. He never backed down and also kept me honest when I went left.

Whenever we are real or are moved to take that leap of faith, some people show up just when you need them. For me, such a person is Moses Mitchell, aka Art of War, Principal, and the primary photographer of a vast majority of the photos. He understood what I tried to explain from my dream and recreated it through the camera lens. His art and vision speak volumes, yet he never uttered a word. Thank you for being an interesting yoga student first, a friend second, and my artist finally.

To Amen, who created an outline that, when I saw it, I believed it could be done. Thank you, Willa Robinson, of KP Publishing, my publisher, for wanting to be a part of this project and making it happen.

To Juan Roberts, of Creative Lunacy, your creative visual genius and talent made us see the light and the visuals of a beautiful layout for *Through My Mother's Eyes*.

Then to friends and family members from all around who shared their stories, their wisdom, and their images to be part of this special project to which we all can relate. I will never forget what you gave me, not just the courage to manifest this piece of myself but also to make it come to life by reminding everyone in the project of who they are, and whose they are.

Finally, and once again, this time by name, I would like to thank my granddaughters, Kelsey and Skyler, as well as my daughters, Alexandria and Chelsea, who remind me of the gift of motherhood. You inspire me to no end.

ABOUT THE VISIONARY

Melba T. Binion-Sanders-Johnson

Melba T. Binion Johnson is a professional actress, model, and author. She has been acting and modeling for the last thirteen years, specifically within the broadcast and print advertising industry. Ms. Johnson is also a 36-year practitioner and senior teacher of Bikram Hot Yoga, as well as a certified Core Power Yoga instructor. Recently, she launched a yoga apparel line called, "It's a Wrap by Melba."

Previously, Ms. Johnson was a co-founder and vice president of Berkhemer Clayton Inc. (aka Diversity Search Partners Inc.), an executive search firm founded in 1993. The firm specializes in recruiting diverse senior-level executives for corporations and institutions throughout the United States. Ms. Johnson served as a partner from 1993 to 2005. During her career, she had the opportunity to speak at the Governor's Conference in California, hosted by former Governors Gray Davis and Pete Wilson. In addition, she has served as both a panelist and a guest speaker for various other conferences, including Leadership America, CareerPath.com, Lee Hecht Harris Outplacement, and Wright Management.

Ms. Johnson served on six non-profit boards in Los Angeles, California, including the Santa Monica College Foundation, Big Sisters of Los Angeles, Daniel Freeman Hospital Foundation, Women's Enterprise Development Corporation (WEDC), Toberman House in San Pedro, and Planned Parenthood, Los Angeles.

Ms. Johnson's other extra-vocational activities have included membership in Women of Los Angeles, Women in Business, Women Incorporated, the Japan America Society, the National Association of Minorities in Cable, Women in Cable Television, and the Cable Television Association of Marketing (CTAM). Her participation with the cable industry groups stems from her experience as a founding partner with HoneyVision, a digital cable network start-up venture in 2000-2001.

Ms. Johnson received her Bachelor of Science degree in Psychology from California State University, Dominguez Hills and is also a graduate of the Fashion Institute of Design and Merchandizing (FIDM), specializing in merchandizing and marketing. Melba Binion Johnson is the mother of five children, grandmother of seven, which include Kelsey and Skyler Yates, co- authors of Twins in (Pairs) Paris. She and her husband reside in San Pedro, California.

Signatures

SIGNATURES

This is Your Page

If I were looking through my mother's eyes, I would see . . .